Why I Love Barthes

Why I Love Barthes

ALAIN ROBBE-GRILLET

Texts collected and edited by Olivier Corpet

TRANSLATED BY ANDREW BROWN

polity

First published in French as *Pourquoi j'aime Barthes* © Christian Bourgois éditeur, 2001, 2009

This English edition © Polity Press, 2011

Polity Press
65 Bridge Street
Cambridge CB2 1UR, UK

Polity Press
350 Main Street
Malden, MA 02148, USA

ISBN-13: 978-0-7456-5078-4
ISBN-13: 978-0-7456-5079-1(pb)

A catalogue record for this book is available from the British Library.

Typeset in 12 on 17 pt ITC Garamond
by Servis Filmsetting Ltd, Stockport, Cheshire
Printed and bound in Great Britain by MPG Books Group Limited, Bodmin, Cornwall

For further information on Polity, visit our website: www.politybooks.com

Contents

Foreword

The friendship between Roland Barthes and Alain Robbe-Grillet began in 1953, with an admiring letter from Barthes to the author of *The Erasers*, telling him of his 'certainty' that this was an '*important* book, an avant-garde book, in a word, a *successful* book'. This relationship, largely owing to the mediation of Jean Cayrol, soon became cordial, and even affectionate, sparking off a real *literary friendship* that lasted twenty-five years.

The text with which this work begins and which gives it its title[1] (suggested by Robbe-Grillet to the organizers of the Colloque de Cerisy devoted to Barthes in 1977)[2] is clear evidence of the extent to which friendship and literature, indissolubly linked, always lay at the heart of their relationship. Robbe-Grillet remained faithful to this friendship until his death: the participants at the last Barthes conference organized by Tom Bishop at New York University in April 2000 still remember the eulogy, full of humour and tenderness, that he improvised that day (his address would have concluded this small volume if any written or audiovisual trace of it had been preserved . . .).

In his last years, sometimes prone to a certain nostalgia, Alain Robbe-Grillet was happy to agree that, while he had enjoyed a full and active social life, his real friends could actually be counted on the fingers of one hand; among these rare elect spirits, after the first and most important of them – his publisher Jérôme Lindon – it was Roland Barthes whom he always mentioned and defended, fiercely if necessary. But over and above this friendship, there was his unfailing intellectual esteem for Barthes. So, in the first volume of his *Romanesques*,

Robbe-Grillet prophesied: 'It's his work as a written author that will last'[3] – an opinion that we can be sure would secretly have delighted Barthes.

In 1995, in the preface to the catalogue of an exhibition in Rio de Janeiro devoted to Barthes's drawings, Robbe-Grillet, under the title 'Yet Another Roland Barthes', imagines Barthes settling down to rewrite *The Sorrows of Young Werther* – maybe with a jubilation similar to that of Robbe-Grillet himself when, a few years later, he indulged in a rewriting of *The Erasers*, in *La Reprise* (2001).

Over the years, in various interviews and lectures, Robbe-Grillet returned to the important role in the reception of his works that had been played by Barthes's articles, published in the reviews *Critique* and *Arguments* and then collected in 1964, in the *Essais Critiques*. At the same time, he never forgot to mention the paradoxical effects of these texts, which confined the

interpretation of his work within a struc-
turalist framework and rhetoric that were
too cut-and-dried for his taste, and thereby
underplayed the contradictions internal to
the work itself, especially the contradiction between its avowed formalism and the
essential place of subjectivity at the heart
of his creative endeavour. These texts by
Barthes, like those by Blanchot or Bataille,
hugely contributed to giving Robbe-Grillet a
dominant position in the literary arena; and
he himself derived the maximum symbolic
benefit from these interpretations, both for
himself and for the other authors of the
New Novel. But after a while he needed,
to some extent, to loosen their grip. For
Robbe-Grillet, the three first texts in this
volume[4] thus represented a belated attempt
to remove an interpretative obstacle which
had in his view, over the years, become a
burden and a distortion. From this point of
view, we might suggest that his insistence
on Barthes the writer is perhaps not alto-

gether separate from his desire to liberate his own work from the marks that Barthes as an essayist had left on it; so the attempts which Barthes made at the end of his life to, shall we say, set himself up as an *'écrivain'* (and not just as a mere *'écrivant'*, to use his own famous distinction)[5] would find in Robbe-Grillet's own attempts a sort of justification or posthumous homage . . .

The fourth text, 'I Like, I Don't Like', was written in autumn 1980, for a commission by France Culture.[6] Twenty years later, this text was so closely associated with the place held by Roland Barthes in Robbe-Grillet's memory that the latter ended up himself believing – and stating[7] – that he had expressly written it the following year, in 1981, on the occasion of a radio homage for the first anniversary of Barthes's death. This was not the case – but does it really matter? This blur of affectionate memories is rather touching, and for that reason we have chosen to close the volume with this text, here published for the first time, firm in our belief that it was composed by Robbe-Grillet at a time when he was thinking of the friend he had lost a few months earlier.

So this is why Robbe-Grillet loved Barthes: because, via what he himself calls a 'shady, suspicious' relationship, it gradually became a 'relationship of novelist to novelist' that built up between them and defined, as he goes on to say, an 'amorous relationship'. So it was two writers, and two friends, whom Christian Bourgois decided to associate in a joint homage, first in 1978, then again in 2002, when he published for his friends a booklet for private circulation reprinting the splendid Cerisy dialogue that opens the present volume. Thirty years later, the exemplary interplay of friendship and what Robbe-Grillet, in *Le Voyageur*, describes as 'the problematic exercise of literature' – where friendship and literature intertwined are mutually necessary to the two men – still forms an essential part of our horizon.

Olivier Corpet

Paris, December 2008

Notes

1 *Pourqui j'aime Barthes'* – *'aimer'*, of course, can be 'like' or 'love', but the warmer verb seems appropriate here (though I have stuck to 'like' in Robbe-Grillet's list of likes and dislikes at the end of this volume). Barthes himself wrote two short essays (1966 and 1974) collected under the title 'Pourquoi j'aime Benveniste', in homage to the great linguist Émile Benveniste, translated as 'Why I Love Benveniste'. – Trans.

2 The château of Cerisy-la-Salle, in Normandy, has long been home to a series of conferences and seminars on contemporary scholarly and intellectual topics. – Trans.

3 In Alain Robbe-Grillet, *Ghosts in the Mirror*, tr. by Jo Levy (London: John Calder, 1988), p. 51. (*Romanesques* is the name Robbe-Grillet gave to his explicitly autobiographical writings – Trans.)

4 These texts, selected and edited by myself

and Emmanuelle Lambert, were brought out together under the title 'Sur Roland Barthes' in Alain Robbe-Grillet, *Le Voyageur: textes, causeries et entretiens, 1947–2001* (Paris: Christian Bourgois, 2001; Points-Seuil, 2003).

5 Barthes drew a precarious and overlapping distinction between an '*écrivain*' and an '*écrivant*': very approximately, the former focuses on language as the site of a creative struggle, while the latter uses it to get things done. – Trans.

6 Robbe-Grillet read this text out in a broadcast on 4 October 1980 in the programme *Mi-fugue, mi-raisin* by Françoise Treussard and Bertrand Jérôme as part of the series 'I Like, I Don't Like' ['*J'aime, j'aime pas*'] (deliberately transformed by Robbe-Grillet for his own text into 'I Like, I Do Not Like' [*J'aime, je n'aime pas*; this latter is a bit more formal. – Trans.]).

7 In particular when the facsimile of the manuscript of this text was published in the illustrated chronology *Alain Robbe-Grillet, le voyageur du Nouveau Roman* (Paris: Éditions de l'Imec, 2002).

Why I Love Barthes
1978

What I must admit, to begin with, is that
I haven't prepared any sort of paper; I've
come here as a friend – a friendly voice
at a conference that now, perhaps, rather
intimidates me. And I have no idea what
I'm going to say. I'd simply like it to be, not
a monologue, but a dialogue, an exchange
between Barthes and myself on a certain
number of points that are close to my heart,
though they're still very vague in my head.
The subject was: why do I love Barthes?

This is the transcription of Alain Robbe-Grillet's talk, and
the ensuing discussion, with Roland Barthes, at the Cerisy
conference on Barthes in June 1977. This talk and the
discussion were published in the conference proceedings
in 1978 (UGE, 10/18), and republished, on the initiative
of Christian Bourgois, in 1978 and 2002, in the form of a
booklet for private circulation reserved 'for the friends of
this publisher'.

1

And this simple utterance is already causing me a variety of problems. The words 'why', 'I love', and 'Barthes' seem almost to require a whole conference all to themselves. First, Barthes. What do I mean by 'Barthes' in the sentence 'I love Barthes'? The fashionable reply, the one which completely eliminates the author, would be this: by 'Barthes' I mean 'Roland Barthes's work'. It's a work that I know well; I've read a great deal of it; I've even learned part of it by heart. (*Laughter.*) Oh, but I have! You know, when I love a writer, I tend not to try to analyse him but to try to learn him by heart. This seems much more important to me. Right now, I can recite Barthes the same way I can recite Flaubert, or Robbe-Grillet. (*Laughter.*) In the contact with the text involved in knowing it by heart, there are things which strike me as crucial. Right now, I still learn texts by heart, as an exercise: last month I learned 'Le Cimetière marin', which is quite something![1] I enjoy doing this: whenever I recite a text, generally in the bath, I have the sense that I'm caught up in a much less absent-minded, much more intimate contact with this text than when I read it. It's a much less absent-minded contact, because I can read it absent-mindedly but I can't easily recite it absent-mindedly. And it's a much more intimate contact because, when I analyse it, I always feel that I'm eliminating the text.

So the word 'Barthes' obviously refers to the writer Barthes. But I also feel strongly that it's something else, too: there's a person there, and not just because I know Roland. Obviously, I've known Roland for a very long time, I know him so well that, to take at random some television programme, for example Pivot's,[2] I say to myself, oh, look, there's Roland chatting away. (*Laughter.*) Obviously, when that happens, the friend ends up eliminating the writer. Not altogether, admittedly. And this is where a first difficulty crops up: I manage less and less to separate the author from the person. So let's try to forget the fact that I know Roland Barthes personally, let's try to forget that the person's a friend. It then becomes apparent that his character as a person (his 'personicity', as Barthes might have put it a few years ago) remains very present in his text. The relationship I have with this text is thus a relationship between one individual and another, one body and another.

In short, it's a shady, suspicious relationship, at least one that's condemned by a whole modernist trend that I still thought worth encouraging even quite recently. And this very powerful way the person intervenes in the text, the sensation that I'm dealing with a body, with bodily drives, with things that aren't clean, probably, means that the text tends to become a mere spokesperson for this body – a perfectly horrible result for someone who, like me, has taken part in this whole endeavour to eliminate the author from his or her text.

So this word 'Barthes' already raises an insoluble problem: there's a contradiction within the word. I'm not going to say that I'm choosing this meaning or that one, or this one with a bit of that one, or 30% text and 70% person: that's impossible. There is, so to speak, not an identity between this person and his text, but, on the contrary, a tense, contradictory relationship. And this means that I can't simply state that Barthes is *in* his text, since he can also appear to me, at any moment, as *against* his text. He and his text form a sort of torsion coupling, which seems to me, on the level of my reading, characteristic of the way I relate, not to a thinker, but to a novelist. In the question 'why do I love Barthes?', Barthes thus assumes the figure of a novelist. He forms the person-text that in my view is very close, for instance, to Flaubert: I can't separate the figure of Flaubert from his texts. I manage to do so for a thinker, in other words for someone whose production seems purely conceptual, but not for a novelist.

And so I come to the second bit of the sentence: 'I love'. In what I've just been saying there already appears a certain nuance to the words 'I love'. My relationship to this work-personage, this text-person, this text-body – a relationship of novelist to novelist – defines a certain type of amorous relationship, of emotional contact.

And then the third word crops up in all its impossibility, the word 'why'. Everything I've just said goes against the notion of 'because'. The entire way I've introduced a certain haziness into those two bits of the sentence, 'Barthes' and 'I love', is going to make the whole idea of 'because' absolutely impossible, and I feel the intense need to replace it by the idea of 'how'. Not 'why do I love Barthes?', but rather 'how do I love Barthes?' How does it feel when one of his texts is going round in my head? How do I live with that text?

Just now, I spoke of a suspicious, even dirty relationship. And there is, after all, something clean in conceptual thinking: a certain virtue, rigour, coherence, totality. Even if conceptual thought trembles, it still aims at a withdrawal of the body. Generally speaking, such thought carries out an act of abstraction so that the whole thing forms a straightforward object, nice and clean, outside my body. If, on the other hand, my body and his body enter into it, then I'm dealing with an object that leaks away on every side, that falls to pieces. From the viewpoint of scientific rigour (since I'm also, in certain aspects of my education and character, a scientist), this object will seem deplorable. In one sense, indeed, I almost miss this lost world of concepts, cleanness, virtue. And perhaps this transition, which I made at the age of thirty or thirty-five, from the scientific to the literary worlds, was precisely a final loss of confidence in virtue and in the possibility of creating a work that would be straightforward, closed, clean and tidy.

In any case, a few years ago, in the way the *Tel Quel* group used the word 'science', and in the elimination of the notion of the author by Jean Ricardou, there was something approaching this idea: a resurgence of the hope of being able to speak in neat and tidy terms, and an increased dislike of the shady contact that the public at large has with literature. How does the public like its literature? Well, you know, it likes it dirty. The popular papers that make a point of discussing the novel, *Le Figaro littéraire* or *Historia* or other publications of this type, are happy to produce articles about the petty sides of great authors. It's very rare for them to get readers excited by pointing out the virtues of their heroes. Far from it: readers seem particularly excited by their weaknesses and failings, almost by the horror that they would quite normally feel when faced by such personalities. These publications, which ordinary people lap up, insist not just on their writers' illnesses – the more salacious ones if possible – but also on their psychological deficiencies. And I guess this is far from being a coincidence. Probably my relationship with the person-text Roland Barthes has to do with, how shall I put it, not his weaknesses, not his failings . . .

Roland Barthes. – . . . His stupidities . . .

Alain Robbe-Grillet. – . . . Stupidities, perhaps, yes, stupidities. When Valéry said 'stupidity is not my forte', there was something funny about it because Valéry actually seemed to have an emotional, fascinated relationship with different kinds of stupidity. And Flaubert too, in *Bouvard and Pécuchet*, right? If you want to say something now, Roland, interrupt me straightaway: I love being interrupted – especially when I've rather lost track of what I'm saying.

Roland B. – If you like, I can drift off from a couple of points, and then you can carry on about the novel. I'm not disagreeing, I'm drifting. In other words, I'm doing what I'd do if you were at my seminar: you present a paper and then I drift off at a tangent. When you said that you recited certain authors' texts, I'd add that, as far as I'm concerned, I don't know anything by heart. I don't know a single text by heart and I'll go so far as to say (quite obviously) not even any of my own. At school, in my day there were still lessons where you had to recite (I don't know if they still exist); this was a test that filled me with terror, and I was never any good at it. I remember that, one day, driving back from Bayonne, as I was alone and it's a pretty long journey (it's a twelve-hour journey on a road I *do* know by heart), I said to myself: okay, I'm going to spend the time learning something by heart; I'd copied out on a piece of paper a fragment from Racine, it was the death of Phèdre, I think, and for twelve hours I tried to learn the death of Phèdre by heart; but I just couldn't do it. When I reached Paris, I'd forgotten all about the death of Phèdre. If I'm telling you this, it's obviously to get beyond anecdotes or remarks about my psychology, and to link this little confession to a theme that Antoine Compagnon brought up in regard to Montaigne, the problem of *amnesia*: as you remember, Montaigne defined himself as outside memory, eluding memory. To give you another anecdote, let me say that, the other day, at the start of this conference, I had a sort of rather terrifying fantasy: I told myself that perhaps I was going to be asked, here, to mention or go over the different stages of my books, the stages of my life, in short that I was going to be asked to remember what I'd written; and this was terrifying because I realized that, basically, I wouldn't be at all able to fulfil this request; so then I invented an allegory: I told myself that, arriving here, we'd crossed a Normandy river called the river *Memory* and that, instead of this place being called Cerisy-la-Salle, it was called Haze-over-Memory. In fact, my amnesia has a character that isn't brutally negative; my memory lets me down, it's a haze. I live in a sort of hazy mist, in the impression that I'm always having to struggle with my memory. It's an idea that could have consequences for writing; writing could be the field of memory's haze, and memory's haze, this imperfect memory that's also an imperfect amnesia, is basically the field of thematics; a theme is something that's both forgotten and not forgotten, and so can't be captured by structural procedures, precisely because it's a phenomenon of intensity, of 'more' or 'less'.

I'll drift off at another tangent, this time more of a question: the presence of the body in my text; Jacques-Alain Miller has mentioned it. I don't think my body is present in my text. I mean that it's a mystery. I don't think, for instance, that my bodily drives run through my text . . .

Alain R.-G. – Your body, for you, but I

was talking about your body for me ...
Obviously, everything I said just now is
something you can't endorse, since, after
all, you're the other ...

Roland B. – You're allowing me to have
a body for myself ...

Alain R.-G. – Yes, of course. (*Laughter.*)

Roland B. – The body is the most imaginary of all imaginary objects.

Alain R.-G. – No, because it finds out-
ward expressions such as the voice, for
example. And the intonations of your voice
are, for me, there in your text ...

Roland B. – Yes, but that's just the point: I
don't recognize my voice. I think they once
carried out this experiment in the United
States: they made a certain number of subjects hear their own voices recorded on
tape without telling them which voice was
which; well, generally speaking, the voice
they didn't like was their own; they had a
feeling of dislike for their own voice. When
I hear myself on the radio, I have a feeling

13

of dislike for that voice, for my voice. The problem, which might be the problem of this conference, would be whether anyone can say, at last, where the violence in my text is. Is it there? It must be, somewhere, but where is it? It's smoothed out here, it's smoothed out there – where is it? Where's the violence in this text?

Finally, there's the resistance to the novel, or at least the problem of the novel. It's a question which very often gets asked in interviews: are you going to write a novel? Now that you're gradually getting closer to novelistic forms, now that the theme of the novel comes up explicitly in what you write, when are you going to write a novel? Go for it, take the plunge [*sautez le pas*]; this expression used to mean (as Gide reminded us) both 'go to a brothel for the first time' and 'take your first communion'. When are you going to take the plunge? When are you going to write a novel? I really want to write a novel, and every time

14

I read a novel that I like, I want to do the same thing, but I seem to have resisted, up until now, certain operations that are supposedly inherent in the novel. For example, the smooth surface, the continuum. Could a novel be written in aphorisms, in fragments? In what conditions? Isn't the very essence of the novel a certain continuum? I think there's a resistance here. The second resistance seems to be the relationship to names, to proper names, I don't know, I wouldn't be able to invent proper names and I really think that the whole novel resides in proper names – the novel the way I read it, of course, and I've said as much in regard to Proust. For the time being, I feel a resistance to inventing names, at the same time that I really want to invent some. Perhaps I'll write a novel the day I invent the proper names for that novel. I've long thought that there was a third resistance, having to use the word 'he', the 'he' of the novel, the third-person character; but I've started to adapt to this difficulty somewhat by mixing 'I' and 'he' in *Roland Barthes by Roland Barthes*. As for the relationship between the figure of the thinker and the figure of the novelist, we ought to take another look at the case of Sartre, who has inevitably made a name for himself as a major 'thinker' and yet has written novels; but he's not viewed as a real novelist.

Alain R.-G. – Well, Sartre's novels are still, probably, badly marred by a kind of formalism, in this sense: he forced himself to write novels the way one *should* write a novel. Sartre had something to express, he was a thinker, and at the same time he said to himself: to get my ideas across, I'm going to write novels. He set out his conceptual thinking in the form of characters and he himself acknowledged that he had failed. So you should especially avoid trying to take the plunge, since I can sense very clearly that some folks are telling you: take the plunge . . .

Roland B. – It's the interviewers . . .

Alain R.-G. – I can easily see how they do it. 'You love *Werther* so much, so tell us Charlotte's story again.' In other words: 'Show yourself to be a complete reactionary with regard to modernity, and reassure us by producing something that conforms to the products that you love in the history of literature'. But that's just what you don't do. And that's where you're right, and that's where you show yourself to be not just a novelist, but a modern novelist, the one who refuses to accept the established order of the novel, the rules of its game, in other words its characters with their names, etc. The problem of the name has been settled for a long time: I myself wrote a novel where there isn't a single proper name, *In the Labyrinth*. Ah, actually yes, there *is* a proper name: Henri Martin, who appears in the last pages and has no relationship with the book. It's perfectly possible to write a novelistic text without a proper name.

17

And if it's important that you don't take the crucial step of accepting the rules, any of them, when it comes to a future novel, this is because the novel has yet again come to a dead end. There was the dead end of Joyce, there was the New Novel of the fifties, which also came to its own dead end, then the New Novel with Jean Ricardou which was called the New New Novel and which has also come to a dead end. Something new needs to be done in the novel, and this something new will be done precisely by someone who refuses to be a professional novelist, to apply any rule at all from the novel of the past. And maybe it will strike future generations that, when all's said and done, the step has already been taken. You didn't do so the way people were expecting you to, by rehabilitating a well-known and perfectly reassuring form, the novelistic novel. With *A Lover's Discourse* you took the step, not the step expected by society, but your own step towards what will

18

appear, perhaps, in twenty years' time, as the New New New Novel of the eighties. Who knows?

Alain Lenoir. – Since you're talking about the novel, I'd like to know whether you reckon Philippe Sollers is already heading that way . . .

Alain R.-G. – But Philippe Sollers has already acknowledged that he's reached a dead end right now, since he's not publishing his *Paradise* in volume form. He says: 'I'm going to wait a while before publishing it.' In my view, there's also been that dead end, but this is merely one of the historical states assumed by the long succession of dead ends in the novel. No, I think that it's something else that people are waiting for. And perhaps they're expecting a novel, a type of novel, that would have a good deal more readers than Sollers's latest experiments. (*Laughter.*) I'm not being mean at all – I don't measure the value of a writer by the number of his or her readers.

However, I do wonder if a certain type of dead end isn't characterized precisely by the total lack of readers – Sollers's dead end lies there. The new opening that might be hoped for, in some unexpected direction (in the general history of what I might call the entropy of the novel, in which literature will one day arrive at its own death, in this ever-changing and exciting landscape), will reveal, I think, a completely new path, quite different from that of Sollers. Of course, this is only my opinion, and I'm saying it entirely for myself. I'm not a man for general truths: I'm talking solely of my personal contacts with literature and, in particular, with Barthes's literature. And the modes of reading that I bring to bear on the novel called *A Lover's Discourse*, on the one hand and, on the other, *Paradise*, as serialized in *Tel Quel*, are fundamentally different for me: for *me*, that is. But what about you, do you think you might read *Paradise* in a similar way and . . .

Alain L. – No, I mean that I don't myself tend to consider Barthes as a novelist . . .

Alain R.-G. – Ah, right. So let me try to explain what I mean by novelist: how, for me, the structure of development of an adventure in a novel relates to the structure of development of a conceptual adventure of thought. This, I think, is the difference between 'trembling' and 'slipping'. Just now I conceded that conceptual thought could tremble, but tremble around a fixed axis; in other words it needs a core of solid meaning that will stop it getting runny, like a Camembert . . . since we're in Normandy. The structure of a slippage, on the other hand, is totally different: it never stops abandoning positions that it pretends to have won. From Barthes's first texts, which I found immensely inspiring, for instance the start of *Writing Degree Zero*, which I could still recite today, I noticed these slippages. In particular, in the rhetorical shape of those fragments of discourse linked together by 'in other words', 'which means that', 'in short', etc. What you have at the start of *Writing Degree Zero* is a series of metaphors concerning language as nature which follow one another in just this way. If we were dealing with a normally organized set of conceptual thoughts, this metaphorical series would increasingly home in on an object whose density would continue to increase; but in fact, when you read this text closely, you realize that it's the complete opposite. You start out from something firm. 'We know that a language is a corpus of prescriptions and habits common to all the writers of a period' (that's clear, that's how it is), and it immediately starts to slip: 'which means that a language is a kind of natural ambience wholly pervading the writer's expression, yet without endowing it with form or content'.[3] This is already a kind of swindle since, in reality, it-doesn't-mean that at all. It's an idea that's slipped, and it's going to keep slipping, from metaphor to metaphor. As a result, in a single page, you won't have found your footing but lost it: the swimmer who thinks he's in shallow waters so he can touch bottom will instead have gradually lost his footing completely, even losing the very notion of footing since he now sees himself floating out in the open sea. From the end of the first page, I'm floating, and if I do hang on to the text as a text I know off by heart, this is because I can't hang on to any firm idea that would be, for me, the essence of the text. No, that text can't be separated out, in Sartre's terms, into a content and a form, I can't find anything in it apart from its form, it has no content other than this kind of slippage that has occurred. And this strikes me as characteristic . . .

Florence Auriacombe. – Starting from this distinction between trembling and slipping, I'm reminded of the theme that's been referred to, the contrast between aphorism and fragment . . .

Alain R.-G. – Yes, I was thinking of that, of course, but I was at the back of the room and hadn't woken up properly, so I didn't speak out, but it occurred to me straightaway.

The Barthesian fragment is always slipping and its meaning lies not in the bits of content that may appear here and there but instead in the very fact of slipping. 'Barthesian thought' (in quotes, since I put thinkers in a different category) lies in slipping and not at all in the elements between which the thought has slipped. At the end of the inaugural lecture Barthes gave at the Collège de France, which I'd really enjoyed, as had the whole audience, though it also aroused a certain hostility among some of the listeners, one young woman, who claimed to be a journalist from *Les Nouvelles littéraires*, really laid into me. While I was voicing all the pleasure I'd derived from the lecture, she burst out, 'But listen, what did he say? Basically he said nothing.' Well, maybe. But there's no contradiction at all between this and the enjoyment I'd had. If I'd been listening to a thinker speak, I'd have been able to sum up the contents of his ideas in a few sentences. I replied, 'Of course not, he didn't say anything, he kept slipping from one fleeting meaning to another equally fleeting meaning.' And it was precisely in this very movement of slippage that resided the functioning of the text, the pleasure I'd taken in listening to it and, for that reason, its importance. The young woman was right, but only from the point of view of someone listening to an intellectual guru who'd come along to deliver a truth, a message. But this was meaningless since, for me, Barthes was, for one thing, a novelist and, for another, a modern novelist. And the modern novelist is distinguished by just this phenomenon: instead of presenting a text, such as a novel by Balzac, that's easy to assemble, gathered in a sphere round its solid core of meaning and truth, the modern novel simply presents fragments which, to crown it all, always describe the same thing – a thing which is almost nothing. But the movement of literature is this slippage from one scene to the same scene that repeats itself in a form that's barely diverted, barely converted, barely inverted . . . I can sense that you don't agree . . .

Roland B. – I do agree, but *you're* the modern novelist.

Alain R.-G. – No, because right now, I'm a novelist of the sixties or seventies, and you're perhaps the one who's going to be the modern novelist of tomorrow . . .

Roland B. – No: after all, we're doing the same thing.

Alain R.-G. True. But that's because, just as Barthes, like any novelist, can only talk about himself, I can only talk about *my*self. That strikes me as important, too. After *Writing Degree Zero*, or more or less at the same time, I read Barthes's texts on *The Erasers* and *The Voyeur* and, at that moment, I had an impression that wasn't at all the sense of some definite truth. I was convinced that Barthes hadn't said anything about me, but quite the opposite, that he was starting to talk to himself, not rigorously, since that would contradict everything I've just said, but in a free-floating way, and that the novelist Barthes was already starting to develop in his texts. I would also draw a distinction between two critics who wrote about my novels in that period, let's say Genette[4] and Barthes. I can see Genette's text on *In the Labyrinth* as a sort of scientific reading of the book. But [R.-G. turns to Barthes – Trans.] your texts on those first two novels are extraordinarily personal. You choose a certain number of elements, which you consume, digest and represent in a completely different form, and this is what fascinates me. Between your text on *The Erasers* and the novel *The Erasers* there is a relationship of novelist to novelist and no longer one of novelist to critic.

Roland B. – In those first two texts, especially in the first, there was still a certain truth, but one of a historical order: I said that in *The Erasers* there was something historically new . . .

Alain R.-G. – Yes, of course . . . but perhaps the thing that was new was you! (*Laughter.*)

Roland B. – But I really don't think . . .

Éric de Marez-Oyens. – This may be a bit of a joke, but in that case we can say that Roland Barthes has just published his first novel . . .

Alain R.-G. – No, he's just published his fifth or his sixth novel.

Roland B. – To move on from this discussion, I'd like to say that your analysis of slippage seems just right to me; it's an analysis of quite remarkable intellectual validity: you rightly picked out those expressions, 'in other words', 'which means that', etc. In fact, the sequence or accumulation of explanations is only ever, in the final analysis, a flaunting of metaphors; the development doesn't enable you to be more accurate, more truthful, from expression to expression, you develop your argument in order to set out metaphors, in other words felicitous expressions, in yet other words, as Blanchot puts it, expressions as various kinds of felicity [*bonheur*]. You set out the expression as something felicitous and this is enshrined in all the 'in other words', 'which means that', etc. On the level of these little operators of discourse, we could take the investigation much further; in one sense, they're merely linguistic tics . . .

Alain R.-G. – No, they're irreplaceable operators of slippage . . .

Roland B. – In that case, the question is: what is the relationship between the linguistic tic and the operator of discourse? We ought to mention a type of writing that never gets discussed, but that had a great importance for me as a seed-bed of these tics [*insémination de tics*] – Michelet's writing. I read a lot of Michelet, I read all of his work, I read him at a time when I hadn't as it were started writing. Michelet's writing had a profound impact on me, it was a seed-bed – in good ways and bad, it has to be said. There are a lot of tics in Michelet, too.

Alain R.-G. – And for me, you know, your first great novel could be *Michelet*. That text of yours was a real achievement . . .

Roland B. – Actually, it's the book of mine which people least talk about and which I can tolerate best.

Alain R.-G. – Oh yes, you'll soon have as many enemies as you have admirers, thank God! After all, a novelist's career can't flourish without enemies . . .

Roland B. – The same goes for an intellectual career.

Alain R.-G. – That's true. (*Laughter.*) So what do people accuse you of? Let's say, for example, that it's cautiousness [*prudence*].

Personally, I easily say things I shouldn't, even if I don't altogether think them, just to annoy people. And when I read you, in *Roland Barthes by Roland Barthes*, for example, I suddenly catch myself thinking, 'Oh dear, he's really not taking any risks here, he's got himself covered on all sides and, yet again, he's sheltered from attack.'

Roland B. – In a television programme in which I happened to be the main character, Jean-Louis Bory said something about me: he didn't attack me, since what he says is always very generous, but he gave me notice as it were, telling me I should at least for once break through this sort of protective coating; he didn't use the word 'cautiousness', I don't know which word he used . . . ah, yes, he wanted me to 'let my hair down' [*caracole*], let my hair down just this once; like all questions, at least the kind asked in France, where questions are nothing other than ways of mentioning yourself, this one was in fact a reference to the man asking it: Jean-Louis Bory was asking me to let my hair down to justify the fact that this is just what *he* does.

Alain R.-G. – And what strikes me as important is precisely that here, too, you don't give in. Just as you don't take the plunge and write Charlotte's story. It's this very cautiousness which is the most magnificent pretext for slippage. You'll have given the impression that you've never taken any risks, and yet you'll have taken people a huge distance away from their point of departure. The method of letting your hair down that consists in arousing disgust in them is a different method, and there's no reason to claim that it's any better than this insidious method. You might well be described as insidious. (*Laughter.*) This isn't in the least an insult, since the very strong presence, in my view, of the texts in question is due precisely to this insidiousness, to the way you'll have made me lose my footing without me seeing exactly where . . .

Roland B. – You even remarked to me just now that the part of the conference that you have attended also seemed too cautious to you . . .

Alain R.-G. – Ah, obviously the master's cautiousness means that the disciples will be cautious too. And the cautiousness of the disciples isn't as interesting, since it doesn't produce anything. Indeed, I can fully justify your cautiousness because it's a text, whereas the cautiousness that you secrete, that you produce around you, among the people who talk to you, has the opposite effect on me. Just as when Roland speaks quietly, so everyone speaks quietly in the conference hall and we'll end up speaking more and more quietly . . .

Roland B. – I don't speak quietly.

Alain R.-G. – You don't speak quietly but you take the precaution of always having a cigarette between your lips, which, as you know, from the point of view of articulation, doesn't allow you to shout things out.

Roland B. – You're as hostile to cigarettes as they are in the United States: Americans can't stand anyone talking to them with a cigarette in their mouth . . . It's a very French habit . . .

Alain R.-G. – Not at all, these are things I find touching. It was this habit that I found touching in Pompidou. (*Laughter.*)

Roland B. – The problem of cautiousness is one I'd like to postpone until this afternoon, since it's the problem of adjectives, of adjectivalization, and it's the problem of the image.

Alain R.-G. – You had something to say, over there . . . Throw caution to the winds!

Roland B. – But speak up, otherwise it'll be my fault.

Florence A. – I can't, and if I can't, it's just because, to some extent, this may be the effect of an ethics which is Barthes's own, and this cautiousness is actually something I fully approve of . . .

Alain R.-G. – But ethics isn't something

you can export: each person forges his or her own ethic, and it's valid only for that person. You have to beware of gurus here too . . .

Michel Serviere. – The insidious person mustn't become an invidious super-ego . . .

Alain R.-G. – That's true. (*Laughter.*) This reminds me of another criticism that keeps going round, too: mastery. And it's not unrelated to the first criticism: the kind of terror that Barthes imposes around himself. (*Murmurs.*) But it's true! You know perfectly well that real terror is the sort you can't see. But I'd rather pick up on a third point: the notoriously 'reactionary Barthes'. There are a lot of people out there who accuse him of only taking an interest, increasingly so, in cultural objects from previous centuries. There was Sollers, true enough, but it's a bit condescending: it's reading 'over his shoulder' and almost 'hit-and-miss', it's like on Jean Daniel, it's all a bit small-scale.[5] But there's a sense that the centre of interest you can really focus well on is a type of music or literature that is, indeed, obsolete; and this shocks people. Well, no. Here again, the opposite is the case: it's essential. If Roland Barthes's critical thinking were a conceptual thinking, regulative, organizing, all-encompassing, he could deal with objects that were slippery. But since his thought is itself slippery, prone to divergences, changes of course, insidious reversals, it needs apparently reassuring objects. It's much more interesting to subject Balzac to slippage than Sollers, since Sollers is already moving in a world of slippages. And I also find it touching that this means you can take an interest in works that I don't find very interesting, such as *The Sorrows of Young Werther*. These texts, which seemed quite solid, are things that you work on, that you manipulate, that you set in motion. And it's much more interesting, for anyone producing slippages, to work on bodies that

seem solid. So I'd turn the criticism round
and say: not at all – this thinking which
seems to circle round cultural objects that
are already well known needs to be seen
as quite the opposite: a way of insidiously
introducing these objects into a modernity
that threatened to elude us. I started to
read Michelet after reading your *Michelet*. I
myself had fallen prey to the Michelet who
had been set up by the Second or Third
Republic, I don't remember which . . .

Roland B. – The Third . . .

Alain R.-G. – The Third, and this was an
object that was constituted in all its solidity,
to be set up as an image to reassure the
republican masses.

Hervé Gaudin. – Did you later use
Michelet's *The Witch*?

Alain R.-G. – When I said that my
Glissements progressifs du plaisir was
an adaptation of Michelet's *The Witch*, it
was actually a free adaptation of Roland
Barthes's *Michelet*. Michelet's ideas do, in

spite of everything, refer to values, while my witch never stops making them slip and getting the meaning to skid from one object to the next. The cinema script ends with the sea breaking on the beach, a bit like the sentence in Paulhan,[6] 'Let's suppose I haven't said anything', that could end all of Barthes's novels. After all these slippages, you withdraw on tiptoe, leaving the scene open for the exercise of a certain freedom – the reader's: after all, if it's impossible for Barthes's thinking to be reactionary, this is because it withdraws. The danger is that it might get set up as the thinking of some master, while it presents itself as a kind of thinking that leaves the field open, which slips in front of you while the text lasts and then withdraws on tiptoes. The exercise of my freedom can remain possible, while this would not be the case if I were dealing with a closed text, whose meaning is constituted once and for all.

Roland B. – It's true that I haven't often

written on the 'modern'. When it comes to the 'modern', you can only carry out tactical-style operations: at certain times you feel it's necessary to intervene to signal some shift in the landscape or some new inflection in modernity. Yes, that's something I really haven't done much . . .

Alain R.-G. – Setting up pointers . . .

Roland B. – I did it for you, at the start; for Sollers I almost didn't need to, I did it maybe once or twice, a while ago now. In the final analysis, that's all I did; perhaps just a little bit for Guyotat;[7] I don't remember very well, my memory's still hazy . . .

Alain R.-G. – No, you also gave Sarduy[8] a few phrases . . .

Ginette Krissing-Berg – For Butor[9] . . .

Roland B. – For Butor, but a long time ago; yes, I did it for Severo Sarduy, but again it was at the start, since, after that, the work keeps going all by itself and, from a tactical point of view, there's absolutely no more room for commentary; indeed, the modern work refuses commentary, it can even be defined as what refuses commentary; this is the first position on the modern. The second reason for abstaining is that I have a stronger and stronger urge to work on the category of the untimely as a force, as a force for displacement, as an energy, a tension; the fragments of *A Lover's Discourse* are presented, from the very first paragraph, as an untimely operation. And lastly, the third reason is that I've suggested a metaphor which accounts for this dialectic of the old and the new, the metaphor of the spiral: things are brought back from the past, but in another place.

Françoise Gaillard. – I merely wanted to say that we mustn't be taken in by this cautiousness in the writing, either, since it strikes me personally, on closer inspection, to show a real lack of caution on the part of Roland Barthes, which I actually enjoy the most: daring to go to the limit of a certain form of naïvety, in the best sense of the term, agreeing to say what people no longer dare to say, or what theory has prevented us from saying. I think that he's the only one with the daring to reinstate what is outdated, and to accept this element of real boldness: daring to say what you don't have the right to say or what you shouldn't say or what it would be ridiculous to say . . .

Alain R.-G. – Hmmm, yeah . . . (*Laughter.*)

Françoise G. – That's where the real risk lies, I think.

Antoine Compagnon – Why the risk?

Françoise G. – The risk of saying what you don't dare say because it seems idiotic to say it. Well, in spite of my own cautiousness, I'm risking saying it . . .

Alain R.-G. – I think that in this case, too, we can't see it as being all of a piece: it's maybe trickier than that. You'll lose a few modernist militants who read things in a rather dumb way, as do all militants, but you'll still win some on the wrong side, if I dare say . . . I felt that very strongly, myself, a few years ago, at a conference on my own modest offerings. (*Laughter.*) In the room there were people who were my intellectual friends, people such as Ricardou, for example, and at every moment I spoke against them, against those friends, because you should always speak *against*. And just then, I felt that I was immediately winning over the approval, in the room, of an old core of reactionaries that you often find hanging around in conference halls (*laughter*), and they were saying, 'We've recuperated Robbe-Grillet.' You should see how happy society is to recuperate Barthes or Foucault. When Foucault, right on the edge of the margins, speaks out very subtly against sexual discourse, you should see how *L'Express*, or even *Le Nouvel Observateur*, publish articles: 'Ah, we're free at last of the tyranny of sex.' I think that, right now, Foucault must feel rather awkward about the interpretations that his book has generated. So the boldness you mentioned, Françoise Gaillard, does exist, but you still need to place it within a general context, that of a society where it won't appear the least bit bold, but quite the opposite. It was wonderful, in *Apostrophes*, when you spoke out, very eloquently and very amusingly, against Françoise Sagan and dear old Madame Golon:[10] 'Yes, but I'm not talking about the same thing, I'm talking of a discourse *on*.' The fact remained that, for those two ladies, as for the audience as a whole, you were saying exactly the same thing as Françoise Sagan. (*Laughter.*) But it's true! After all, I live in the countryside, with peasants who listen to Pivot's programmes, and I see the kind of reaction that people have who've not read you [Barthes] or Sagan.

Roland B. – But I have absolutely nothing against Françoise Sagan . . .

Alain R.-G. – Neither do I: what I'm saying is that there's a risk that you might seem to have a similar position. But in my view, your positions are fundamentally opposed. Still, this magnificent career that you're enjoying proves that it all paid off. (*Laughter.*) Ah, I don't mean it was all planned . . . (*Laughter.*)

Alain L. – I'd like to know if Robbe-Grillet knows Roland Barthes's text, in *Tel Quel* no. 47, on stereotypes?

Alain R.-G. – Oh yes, but I can't recite it, unfortunately. Can *you* recite it?

Alain L. – No, I don't know it off by heart, but anyway, I just wanted to say that this great load of never-ending stereotypes that we've been hearing over the past half hour leaves me uneasy . . .

Alain R.-G. – Do you think that we can talk with anything other than stereotypes?

Alain L. – Roland Barthes has proved that we can . . .

Alain R.-G. – Maybe I'd say that he handles them more skilfully. But you seem to be reacting rather emotionally, as if I was attacking Roland Barthes. I may be wrong . . .

Alain L. – No, it doesn't have to do with Roland Barthes, but with the whole set-up; this is going to appear a bit off the subject, but anyway, I feel there's a whole theatrical side to this intervention, as if there was a certain desire to force a break somewhere . . .

Alain R.-G. – *I* don't want to force a break, I wasn't here before . . .

Alain L. – It's like witnessing someone trying to force a break and failing . . . (*Laughter.*)

Alain R.-G. – Maybe it's a personal allergy of yours. The term 'failure' can only be used with a statistical weight. What you are perhaps within your rights in saying is probably that there's something not quite right between you and me . . .

Alain L. – It's not as simple as that. When I say 'theatrical' I also mean 'seductive'.

Alain R.-G. – Ah, so it's me that's

45

seductive? . . . (*Laughter.*) Personally, it's Barthes that I find seductive . . .

Alain L. – Roland Barthes has a talent for slippage, but I think that you, Robbe-Grillet, share it.

Jean Crocq. – You can slip, but you can't really let go. At the start, when Robbe-Grillet erupted into this room, you could feel a kind of urge to distance himself more definitely. There certainly is in Robbe-Grillet right now a desire to move away from Barthes, but he's not taking this to its logical conclusion. At any rate, when we talk of slippage, we're in the realm of metaphor, the metaphor of a certain trembling; from a conceptual style of thought that aims at rigour, via glissando after glissando, you end up in a kind of generalized muffle; someone just now mentioned a muffled atmosphere . . .

Alain R.-G. – Yes, I rather felt that I'd left my earplugs in . . .

Jean C. – It would be a good idea for

Barthes to be 'placed' to some degree right now . . . personally, I'd say that Barthes is in a period of retreat. He's experiencing a kind of false 'high point' of recuperation. He's the representative of what might be called soft modernity (*laughter*): writing to be savoured. Ultimately, we're still in something sleek and smooth, and behind Barthes's fragmentations, there's an underlying smoothness, a glissando that doesn't catch onto anything. In spite of all this, a more definite kind of distancing might be desirable. Glissando is acceptable, and slippages, but cleaner breaks are in order. We're all immersed, so to speak, in a kind of seed-bed [*insémination*] where the muffled atmosphere spreads everywhere. (*Murmurs.*)

Alain R.-G. – When I said 'why I love Barthes' (I didn't manage to get that far because, luckily, it turned into a dialogue), I wanted to emphasize that, in his texts, there's a violence that speaks to me

47

directly, something where the differences between his cautiousness and my letting-my-hair-down are considerably lessened. Here too, the reason why I love reciting a text is because it's when I recite it that I can reconstitute all its violence. It's when it erupts as text that its violence is made manifest. Whereas in a muffled conference like the one you've mentioned, there's going to be a sense that this violence hasn't disappeared but has completely changed face.

Patrick Mauriès. – Yes, but I feel that's just it: you yourself haven't faced your violence. You started to say: the texts I love are the ones that I learn by heart, I don't analyse them, and three minutes later you did a stylistic analysis . . .

Alain R.-G. – Of course. You have to contradict yourself, otherwise there's no slippage. I also indulge, from time to time, in the activity of teaching literature, at New York University, and I'm always having to face this problem: how can I talk about the text without moving outside it? I've given classes on Barthes, on Pinget,[11] on film directors I like, and the first thing I do is to read, or get someone else to read, the text out aloud, or else I show the film, so that the text is the starting point. Then there's a series of conceptual investments which go deep into the text, interrupted by new readings, as if it were necessary to mistrust this conceptualization that would otherwise make us forget the text as violence, since an idea is never as violent as a text, an idea is always reassuring insofar as it is an idea, insofar as the idea will inevitably adopt the mode of elocution of the existing society. I can only think in terms that ideologically fit in with the society in which I live, but I can, against that way of thinking, produce textual objects, and *these* will be a form of violence.

Patrick M. – It strikes me that violence can only be shown indirectly: you can't confront violence, and you've demonstrated as much in your demeanour; otherwise, it turns into a hysterical happening . . .

Alain R.-G. – Absolutely. How to talk about literature while leaving its violence intact. As soon as I start talking about it, this violence vanishes. And in any case, when we talk about recuperation by the universities, every academic discourse, even when it's modernist, will bring works that had tried to elude it within the established order of conceptualization. Obviously, the most magnificent example to hand is Sartre's *Genet*, where Genet becomes someone who operates along the lines . . .

Roland B. – Personally, I consider that it's Sartre's finest book . . . I profoundly admire this book . . .

Alain R.-G. – But Genet's violence is no longer there . . .

Roland Barthes's Choice
1981

Was Roland Barthes a thinker? This question immediately leads to another one: what is a thinker, these days? Not so long ago, a thinker was deemed to provide his fellow citizens with certainties, or at least a few definite lines, constant, inflexible, able to sustain his own discourse and thereby to guide the thought and conscience of his era. A thinker was a master, a *maître à penser*. Definiteness was his essential quality, his status.

Barthes was a thinker of slippage. After his inaugural lecture at the Collège de France, while I was voicing my enthusiasm

---

Text published under this title in *Le Nouvel Observateur*, no. 855, 30 March–5 April 1981, partly reprinted in *Ghosts in the Mirror*, tr. by Jo Levy (London: John Calder, 1988), pp. 50–5, and here newly translated.

for the performance, a young girl I didn't know pounced on me, vehement and angry: 'What do you admire in all that? From start to finish, he didn't say *a thing*!' This wasn't altogether accurate; he'd not stopped saying things, but he'd taken care that this didn't congeal into *something*: using the method he had been perfecting for many years, he had withdrawn from what he was saying as he said it. To stymie the provocative formula he'd come up with, which set so many tongues wagging that evening, when he stated that all language is 'fascist', he provided us with the disturbing example of a discourse that wasn't: a discourse which destroyed within itself, step by step, all temptation of dogmatism. And what I particularly admired in this voice, which had just kept us in suspense for two hours, was the way it left my freedom intact: or even more, that it gave it, at each new turn of the phrase, new strength.

Dogmatism is nothing other than the

discourse of truth. The traditional thinker was a man of truth, but he could believe in all good faith that the reign of the true marched alongside all progress in human freedom, hand in hand together. A fine utopia, a fine fraud, which lit up the euphoric dawn of our bourgeois society, as did a little later the dawn of infant 'scientific' socialism. Alas, today we know where *that* science leads. Truth, in the last analysis, has never served anything but oppression. A century of hopes, of wrenching disappointments and bloody paradises has at least taught us to mistrust it: 'I'm voting for the Socialist Party candidate,' a friend of mine who is a sociologist says, 'since at least he doesn't have any particular policies.'

The slippings and slidings of this eel (Barthes, I mean) are not due to chance, nor to any weakness of judgement or character. Far from it. Words which change, head off in another direction, turn round – that is his lesson. So our last 'true' thinker will have been the one before: Jean-Paul Sartre. *He* wanted to enclose the world in a totalizing (totalitarian?) system worthy of Spinoza and Hegel. But at the same time, Sartre was haunted by the idea of freedom, and this is – thank God – what undermined whatever he set out to do. So his great constructions – novels, critiques, or works of pure philosophy – all remained unfinished, open to all the winds.

From the point of view of his plans, Sartre's work is a failure. And yet, it is this failure that we now find so exciting. He wanted to be the last philosopher, the last thinker of totality, but in the final analysis he will have been in the vanguard of new structures of thinking: uncertainty, instability, drifting. And it then becomes clear how the words 'useless passion' that ended *Being and Nothingness* were not that far removed from Jean Paulhan's 'let's suppose I haven't said anything', which seemed to be a world away.

In 1950, Barthes arrived on this landscape which we can already see to be a thinking in ruins. And, curiously, he initially hitched his own ideas to the reassuring work of Marx. In a quarrel with Albert Camus on *The Plague*, he shut up that humanizing moralist with a lofty 'historical material-ism', as if this were some tried and tested value. But soon, he gradually withdrew from Marxism, quietly and without fuss, on tiptoe as always.

Big new systems of thought lured him: psy-choanalysis, linguistics, semiology. Hardly had the label of semiologist been stuck to him than he started to hate it. Openly mock-ing 'our three policemen: Marx, Freud and Saussure', he ended up severely criticizing the intolerable imperialism of any power-ful system, in his celebrated apologia for the chip-pan: a 'truthful' discourse, one that hangs together too consistently, is like boil-ing oil – you can dip whatever you like into it, what comes out will always be a chip.

Barthes's work, on the other hand, never denies its past, and this is because this ever-renewed movement, moving itself out of itself, this movement constitutive of freedom (which can never become an institution since it exists only in the moment of its own birth), is exactly what he had been pursuing since forever, with the greatest passion, from Brecht to Bataille, from Proust to the New Novel, from the reversals of the dialectic to the analysis of fashion. Like Sartre when he started out, Barthes rapidly discovered that the novel or the theatre, much more than the essay, is the natural place for concrete freedom to come into play with the most violence and effectiveness. The novel is already, as it were, the becoming-world of philosophy. Was Barthes, in turn, a novelist? This question immediately leads to another one: what is a novel, these days?

Paradoxically, in the fifties he took my own novels as infernal machines that enabled him to spread terror; he went on to endeavour to reduce their insidious slippages, the ghosts between their lines, their self-erasure and their gaps, to a 'thingly' [*chosiste*] universe that, instead, affirmed only its own solidity, objective and literal. Of course, that aspect was admittedly present in the books (and in my theoretical remarks), but as one of the two irreconcilable poles in a contradiction. Barthes took the decision to turn a blind eye to the monsters hidden in the shadows of the hyperrealist painting. And when the ghosts, in *Last Year in Marienbad*, invaded the screen too obviously, he moved away.

I think that he himself was struggling with similar contradictions. In *The Erasers* and *The Voyeur*, he refused to see either the spectre of Oedipus Rex or the obsession with sexual crime, since, struggling against his own ghosts, he needed me only as a kind of spring-cleaning. As a good terrorist, he had merely chosen one of the ridges of the text, the sharpest, to wield me as a kind of weapon. But in the evenings, once he'd come down off the barricades, he would go home to wallow ecstatically in Zola, his over-rich prose and his gravy of adjectives . . . Even though he also criticized the way I described snow in my *Labyrinth* for being too 'adjectival'.

Ten years later, he enthusiastically latched on to the publication of my *Project for a Revolution in New York*, which he saw as being as perfect as a 'Leibnizian model', albeit a mobile one. None of this solves the big question: what novels would he have written himself? He discussed this more and more, publicly as well as privately. I don't know whether there are any drafts or fragments in his papers. In any case, I'm certain it wouldn't have been *The Erasers* or *Project*. He said he could only write a 'real novel', and he mentioned his problems with the past historic and the proper names of the characters. In an even more disconcerting change of direction than the previous ones, it seemed that the literary landscape around him had gone back to that of the end of the nineteenth century . . .

And why not? Nobody should define *a priori* the direction taken by research. And Barthes was subtle and wily enough to transform, yet again, that apparently real novel into something completely new, perplexing, unrecognizable.

Yet Another Roland Barthes
1995

Roland Barthes did not love himself. Or rather, perhaps, he loved himself too much, with a love that was too demanding and constantly disappointed. I have already repeated – I can't remember where – what he one day told me on this subject: 'The main difference between me and you is that you have a good relationship with your imago.' I have often wondered whether this wasn't also an unfavourable judgement he was passing on me, or at least a reservation, which means that we were never really intimate, in spite of our friendship. Anyway, it strikes me as

---

Text published in the catalogue of the exhibition of Roland Barthes's drawings (*Roland Barthes artista amador*) at the Museum of the Cultural Centre of the Banco do Brasil, in Rio de Janeiro, between April and September 1995.

obvious that this fundamentally unhappy relationship which he suffered from when it came to any image of himself, whether it was the image reflected in a mirror, or the representation which others formed of him, this terror of seeing his self [*moi*] coagulate, this neurotic refusal to assume a shape, played an essential role, not just in his emotional life, but also in his work as a whole.

When I got to know him in 1953, in other words just after the publication of *The Erasers*, he was the herald, the angel of the annunciation declaring the arrival of a pure, dry literature, disembodied, as it were, and the exact opposite of his own sensual tastes that naturally inclined him towards the over-rich adjectival style of Zola. The apparent austerity of my first published novels must have helped him to fight against his own demons – a slimming programme, as people called it at the time. It is highly likely that if Roland had been able to read *A Regicide*, my first novel (though it was published much later), he would have been more cautious: the poetic way I write about tender flesh and lowering mists would probably have made him fear a rapid resurgence (one that became evident after *Jealousy*) of subterranean forces that he had hitherto forced himself to ignore, despite their constant presence between the lines of *The Erasers* and, even more, *The Voyeur*. The luring song of the little siren-like adjectives, in this first text, *A Regicide*, would immediately have obliged him to tie himself to the mast of his all-too-fragile battleship. I attempted a succinct analysis of these misunderstandings in the first volume of my *Romanesques*, *Ghosts in the Mirror*. I have just used the word 'fragile'. Yes, paradoxically, while he presented to everyone (with his imposing stature, his measured movements, his benevolent half-smile) the external appearance of someone who easily dominates things, even when they go against him, thanks to the quiet strength of reason, Roland Barthes made no secret of a strangely vulnerable fragility. One evening, at a dress rehearsal in a big Paris theatre, we met up with him in the interval. Catherine [R.-G.'s wife – Trans.], without the least bit of malice, asked him a gentle, innocent question about the very mediocre pamphlet attacking him that had just been published, claiming to demystify the total fraudulence of his writing, and creating a real stir in the milieu of Saint-Germain-des-Prés. A similar lampoon that had come out a few years earlier, laying into me, had given me considerable delight. But it was quite the opposite with Roland. His expression changed completely and, to the stupefaction of Catherine, who felt utterly sheepish about it all, he vehemently declared to her that he wouldn't read this book, fearing that, if he did, he wouldn't ever be able to write another line again! The impression of serenity that his whole physical demeanour created – including on that particular day – seemed to give the lie to such an exaggerated response. And yet, in spite of appearances, he was not joking.

So was the imperturbable body that he presented to the world merely one last hoax? Of course not! For it was this very body that he hated most passionately: the august silhouette of a Roman senator seemed to him to be all tangled up in the folds of his toga, that handsome, reflective face, which combined the friendly consideration of Socrates with the wisdom of Buddha, was in his view merely the clearly identifiable mix of an incurable flabbiness of character with the premature plumpness of a pleasure-seeker. When he looked in the mirror, all he saw was spinelessness, a double chin, and cowardice.

And it goes without saying that he loathed all the photographs that exposed him to the gaze of others, in the media. There are many professionals working for agencies or newspapers who can still remember the problems caused by the sittings that he sometimes accepted, out of duty, kindness or resignation. But apart from the images that represented him in his role as a writer, he felt strong positive emotions (empathetic, fascinated) when he encountered traces of the past, even the quite recent past, left behind by photographers, especially amateurs. This apparent contradiction is easily explained: photography belongs to the domain of death, the death of friends or parents, or of anonymous lives from former days, the death of the things of life, the death of the instant which was innocently passing by only to be suddenly slain by the click of the camera. To see oneself dead is acceptable only in the snapshots of childhood, of school, of military service or other bygone periods of our age. Roland could not, without feeling sick, contemplate himself as dead at any precise moment of the previous week, unless he had by some miracle managed, that day, to resemble the death mask of Pascal.

At his last seminars in the École des Hautes Études, his considerable – and contagious – success meant that the lecture rooms were always too small. One morning, it got so crowded that faithful devotees had added a great number of extra chairs, not only at the foot of the lectern but also, this time, on either side of it. When Barthes took his seat, he immediately realized that some spectators could see him from the side, and even from three-quarters behind. Seized by panic, he stood up and had the room cleared. He himself told me this anecdote: he could not stand being examined this way, in profile, for two solid hours. Face to face with another person, he hoped he would be able to dominate his facial expressions. But he knew that his profile would be defenceless, offered up to onlookers who themselves would be safely sheltered, as if behind a two-way mirror in a brothel: unseen, uncaptured, solitary and invulnerable.

Here too, however, this unhealthy

mistrust of his own body, always suspected of insidiously betraying him, went together with a carnal intelligence which led him towards the body in general, its vital functions, sensuality, an appetite for the world. Living is an exercise of the body as well as an adventure of the mind, and these aspects are inseparable. But while, as Descartes put it, when it comes to the mind 'the very people who are the most difficult to satisfy in every other respect do not usually wish for more common sense than they actually have', there is no lack of people who would wish to have, for their own bodies, more slimness, agility, strength, health, endurance, and so on and so forth . . . and more youth, of course, especially in the case of ageing adults. Roland liked the mind's body and the body's mind. What he so disliked, indeed hated, in himself was something like the body's body, the body glued into its sticky corporeality, hunkered down in its flabbiness, its treachery, its fat, its gooey thickness, like a yellowish, viscous pap – the complete opposite of a crystallization.

Of course, his relationship to food was the site of his most painful confrontations. Sometime in the mid-fifties, in Brest, my mother handed me a letter that the postman had just delivered. After a brief glance at the handwritten superscription, she informed me, as if the thing were self-evident, that my correspondent liked fatty foods. My mum was not a specialist in graphology, and I was pretty amazed at her trenchant conclusion, which, as I later verified, was not altogether wrong. However, just a few years later, I read – to my extreme surprise – something my friend had written: in a restaurant, he said, it is the menu that people enjoy consuming – not the dishes, but their description. Lo and behold, he had relegated the whole art of cooking – which he adored – to the status of an abstract exercise of vocabulary!

As I have said, we can find in Barthes's

intellectual speculations, throughout his career, this permanent dread of coinciding with himself in a kind of reconciled self-satisfaction. He would apply Marxist arguments, barely qualified, and with a certain elegance, to social observation; he would even crush the unfortunate Albert Camus with the sledgehammer of an authoritarian reference to historical materialism – and yet he would quickly protest at the label 'Marxist' that people felt they could apply, quite innocently, to him. Over the years, he followed the meandering course of dialectical materialism, psychoanalysis and linguistics, but soon went on to denounce the dictatorship of 'our three policemen: Marx, Freud and Saussure'. Barthes handled the art of discourse with obvious pleasure and perverse skill, but then claimed that all language was 'fascist'.

Indeed, he was to remain, in my view, the patent inventor of a curious figure of rhetoric. He pretended he was trying to catch some thought precisely in his writing, but in the same proposition he would juxtapose successive, more or less metaphorical approaches that seemed to converge on some final meaning; then, as if to clinch matters, he would state, 'in short, it's a whole . . .' followed by a term that unfortunately sends us off, all at once, towards a completely different and even entirely antagonistic order of interpretation. He would create the impression that he was giving the avid reader a final assurance, the key to the entire system (the word that would sum up all the rest), only to shake the reader with a brutal jolt; having lured this over-confident novice right up to the threshold of a definitive meaning, just on the final spurt he would trip him up, sending him gliding out above sudden gulfs.

But I've already started to feel afraid, over the past few paragraphs, of sensing the hatred of my old friend, who died prematurely: Roland's ghost, reading the present preface over my shoulder as I write it, has caught me out in a blatant breach of honour, dipping his still-warm remains into the 'chip-pan' that he so fiercely denounced while he was alive: Barthes was this, Barthes reacted like that . . . So I now turn towards him, with a knowing and humorous wink, but to appease him I must here bring my enterprise to a halt. I have no right to dissect my former comrade-in-arms like this, more or less clumsily. However, I am reserving the right to invent him now in my own way, quite openly.

So: one fine morning, Barthes does indeed take the plunge, as a result, not of any sudden revelation, but rather of a slow process of ripening that has come to an end: he must write a novel, a conceivable text that can allow itself to be a multi-dimensional space in which those countless insoluble contradictions will restlessly circulate.

Now he gets up early, impatient and cheerful, and immediately settles down to work. His pen glides across the white page, in a state of euphoria, with inexhaustible zest. He thinks he has a 'style' rather than a 'writing' [*écriture*] (in the 1950s sense), and this brings a smile to his lips: but he couldn't care less. Style, he admitted to me during a discussion of the jury for the Prix Médicis (of which he was briefly a member – in those days they used to meet in the home of Edgar Faure, at the Hôtel de Lassay), style, as you know, is the only thing that counts; his hero is young and handsome, disabused, romantic. His name is Rolla. The story takes place in the south of Brazil, during the reign of Dom Pedro II, the last emperor. It is a paradoxical landscape, where on the same plot of land there mingle the gnarled vine stock and the luxuriant leaves of the banana trees, with their thick, insubstantial stalks, and where wild orchids grow on chestnut trees in a specious Creole mildness. The heroine, barely out of adolescence, is called Charlotte, in memory of a young German friend, Carl Ott, who endows the fictitious character with his attractive androgynous face and several traits of a whimsical, contradictory, often unpredictable character.

But the author now realizes that he is rewriting *The Sorrows of Young Werther*, and finds this amusing. Isn't rewriting an integral part of his motives? In any case, war has broken out again on the borders with Paraguay, and his hero, constantly transforming, is now called Laurent (sometimes spelled Loran, or Lorào); he covers himself with glory and military panache, dashing on his white charger from headlong charge to single combat, while continuing to sow increasing havoc among the hearts of his admirers. Charlotte suffers the pangs of jealousy and flies on horseback from the home of her legitimate spouse, who has turned suspicious, anxious and cruel. Disguised as a soldier, she joins a company of scouts. She finds her wounded lover in an old half-ruined Spanish fortress overlooking the Rio Grande do Sul. He has assumed the name Horla, while his real name is Orlando, but it is a mixture of *Tristan* and the *Château des Pyrénées*[12] that our polyanecdotal novelist appears to be busily rewriting.

In any case, the subject of his narrative is not the adventure, but the physiology and psychology of his touching protagonists. In his test tubes he analyses their unstable behaviour, their somatic problems, their ambiguous words, their secret feelings, like a chemist in the cosy refuge of his laboratory. And there is no risk of any explosion. As is well known, Barthes remarked (in connection with Pasolini) that the word 'shit' does not smell at all, but he also realizes that the wounds of his heroes, whether they are inflicted on body or soul, harm nobody, not even themselves.

Now, at meal times, he can eat everything he fancies, and as much as he wishes. The old problems have vanished here, too.

Every evening, he goes out, just as he used to, to the liveliest clubs in Paris, the trendiest, noisiest ones: *Palaces* for cruising and romance, where he moves around without touching the ground, as if levitating.[13] All his friends are there, the new ones, the old ones, the next ones, the future indeterminate ones. The situation has changed, for good. Although he is personally involved, he experiences it as if it were a scene from his book, from the same distance, both understanding and filled with affection.

At night, having returned to his citadel, he plays music there for hours on end, just for himself. He has abandoned the piano, as well as the guitar. He now plays the cello. His hours are no longer numbered – time seems to have broadened out, in every direction. Tomorrow, he'll probably get back to his painting, but he will follow an entirely new path . . .

I Like, I Don't Like
1980

I like life, I don't like death.

However, I quite like things that remain motionless (I like cats, I don't like dogs). I like the sense of eternity, old provincial mansions with their changeless furnishings, the heavy red velvets that have always been faded, the moss on the garden paths, the drifting carp in the ponds.

I don't like the telephone. I don't like cars. I like long journeys by train: Paris–Bucharest, New York–Los Angeles, Istanbul–Tehran, Moscow–Vladivostok.

I also like walking, down streets or across the countryside. I like damp, mild

Text written in autumn 1980 for a commission from France-Culture.

autumns, the brown leaves shining with raindrops, lying in a squelching carpet on the roads.

I don't like noise. I don't like bustle. I like beautiful voices. I hate people shouting.

I like enthusiastic crowds. I don't like what crowds like. I don't trust the masses.

I like the days when I feel more intelligent, better educated, sharper. I like learning. I like teaching.

I don't like giving a conference paper after a good meal. I like red wine. I don't like scotch. I like the French language.

I like life. I like literature.

I don't like . . . the three dots of an ellipsis. I don't like thinking about what I don't like.

I liked Roland Barthes's voice.

I do like young girls, especially if they are pretty; I don't really like young boys.

I like pretty things. I don't like the fashion for ugliness.

I like saying what I think, especially if

it's not the done thing to say it. I don't like militants, of whatever tendency.

I like knowing the rules. I don't like respecting them.

I like small things. I like the streets of New York, the vast landscapes of the American West. I don't like big words.

I like understanding. I like analysing things. I like knowing about theories, whether literary or scientific.

I like freedom. I don't like waste. I don't like journalists' lying claptrap.

I like my mum and dad. I mistrust psychoanalysts.

I like to annoy people. But I don't like people to damn well annoy me.

Translator's Notes

1 'The Cemetery by the Sea', a long poem (144 lines) by Paul Valéry, published in 1920.

2 Bernard Pivot, French journalist, ran the weekly TV programme *Apostrophes* (1975–90), on which writers appeared to discuss their work.

3 Roland Barthes, *Writing Degree Zero*, tr. by Annette Lavers and Colin Smith (London: Jonathan Cape, 1984), p. 11.

4 Gérard Genette (b. 1930), great French narratologist and poetician who was associated with structuralism; he and Barthes wrote supportively of each other's work.

5 A (jokey) reference to Barthes's book *Sollers Writer* in which Barthes suggested various ways of reading Sollers's texts. Jean Daniel was the founder of *Le Nouvel Observateur*.

6 Jean Paulhan (1884–1968), French writer, critic and editor of the *Nouvelle revue française*, and a colleague of Barthes.

7 Pierre Guyotat (b. 1940), French writer, some of whose remarkable avant-garde texts dealt with the Algerian war, homosexuality, and other taboo subjects, and were long banned; he was supported by Barthes and many other intellectuals.

8 Severo Sarduy (1937–93), Cuban poet and playwright, praised by Barthes for his 'baroque' style.

9 Michel Butor (b. 1926), French novelist and essayist on an encyclopaedic range of (mainly literary) subjects. Barthes wrote admiringly of his more experimental work and saw him as having affinities with structuralism.

10 Françoise Sagan and Anne Golon were both popular novelists.

11 Robert Pinget (1919–97), French avant-garde writer, translated by Beckett and associated with the New Novel movement in France.

12 *Le Château des Pyrénées* seems to be a reference to the work of that name by Frédéric Soulié (1800–47), whose novels were as celebrated in the nineteenth century as those by Balzac and even Eugène Sue. It is also the name of Magritte's famous painting.

13 Barthes was an habitué of *Le Palace*, Paris's hottest nightspot in the 1970s.